EGYPT TRAVEL GUIDE 2025

Expert Guidance on Safety, Transportation, Accommodation, Culture, Cuisine and Nile River Cruises

BY

GEORGE J HUMPHREY

EGYPT TRAVEL GUIDE 2025: Expert Guidance on Safety, Transportation, Accommodation, Culture, Cuisine and Nile River Cruises

TABLE OF CONTENTS

1. INTRODUCTION

Egypt, the land of pharaohs and pyramids, has always been charming. Nestled in the northeastern corner of Africa, Egypt is a country with a rich cultural heritage intertwined with ancient history and breathtaking scenery. The magnificent Nile River provides food and water to the nation. In this comprehensive analysis, we set out to uncover Egypt's essence, from its remarkable past to its vibrant present.

Egypt is a country of extreme contrasts, where the modern and the ancient coexist. Massive cities, bustling marketplaces, and vibrant street life stand in stark contrast to the timeless grandeur of its archaeological treasures. A sensory extravaganza awaits visitors who wish to delve further into Egypt's mysteries, from the bustling streets of Cairo to the well-known pyramids of Giza.

1.1 Historia and Culture: The Course of Civilization

Egypt's history spans more than five millennia, making it one of the oldest civilizations in the world. The astounding architecture, intricate hieroglyphics, and profound religious ideas that the ancient Egyptians left behind continue to captivate people worldwide.

The ancient Egyptians produced massive structures like the Great Pyramid of Giza and the Sphinx with remarkable accuracy, demonstrating their leadership in science, medicine, and engineering. They worshipped gods and goddesses, and their daily lives were filled with rituals and rites centered upon this.

Throughout history, Egypt has experienced the influence of several civilizations, such as the Greek, Roman, Arab, and Ottoman empires, all of which have left their cultural and historical marks. Egypt's diverse history and influences are reflected in the country's intricate tapestry of festivals, music, art, and cuisine. Today, customs are a melting pot.

1.2 Ecology and Terrain: From the Nile to the Sand Dunes

The main feature of Egypt's topography is the Nile River, which rises in the north from the center of Africa and feeds the surrounding area. It has sustained civilization for millennia. The enormous Sahara Desert, which occupies much of Egypt's landscape, contrasts strongly with the lush greenery and abundant animals of the fertile Nile Delta.

The Nile River is an important aspect of Egyptian culture and daily life in addition to being a lifeline for transportation and agriculture. Egypt's past is still evident along its banks, where thriving cities, stunning tombs, and ancient temples can be seen.

Egypt has a mostly desert environment with warm, dry summers and moderate winters. The climate is more temperate and features more humidity and colder temperatures toward the Mediterranean shore. Oases dot the desert environment, where luxuriant vegetation and date palms thrive in the dry conditions.

Egypt has had environmental difficulties recently, such as pollution, water scarcity, and the consequences of climate change. In order to ensure that future generations may continue to appreciate the beauty and abundance of this historic land, efforts are being made to solve these problems and encourage sustainable development.

Egypt is a country of striking contrasts where both historical wonders and contemporary marvels coexist peacefully. Egypt provides a voyage of discovery unlike any other, from the ageless magnificence of its archaeological monuments to the dynamic vitality of its cities. Egypt is a destination that is guaranteed to make an effect on everyone who visits, whether they want to explore the mysteries of the pyramids, cruise the timeless waters of the Nile, or immerse themselves in the rich tapestry of Egyptian culture.

2. PLANNING YOUR TRIP

Traveling to Egypt is an exciting excursion that offers a wealth of historical and contemporary treasures. However, to guarantee a seamless and pleasurable experience, careful planning is necessary. We go over all the important details of organizing a vacation to Egypt in this comprehensive guide, including when is the ideal time to go and important health and safety advice.

2.1 Seasonal Considerations: When to Go

Selecting the ideal time to visit Egypt can make all the difference in the world to your trip. There are two distinct seasons in the nation: a moderate, milder winter from October to April, and a hot, dry summer from May to September. The best seasons to visit Egypt's outdoor attractions and archaeological sites are in the spring (March to May) and fall (September to November), when temperatures are good and there are less tourists.

Summertime in the United States can be scorching, with highs surpassing 40°C (104°F) in many places, especially the desert regions. But this time of year also happens to be the off-peak travel season, so you might be able to discover better rates on lodging and excursions.

Winter, on the other hand, offers more moderate temperatures and pleasant weather for visiting outdoor monuments like the Giza, Luxor, and Aswan pyramids. But keep in mind that this is also the busiest travel season, so budget for more crowds and more expensive lodging.

The ideal time to travel to Egypt ultimately depends on your tastes and objectives. Making the most of your trip can be facilitated by smart planning, regardless of your preference for avoiding crowds or taking advantage of milder weather.

2.2 Visas and Requirements for Entry: Crucial Details

It is imperative that you become familiar with the entry criteria and visa restrictions prior to your trip to Egypt. The majority of travelers to Egypt need a visa, which can be obtained at the airport or in advance from an Egyptian embassy or consulate.

Certain nationals may be able to enter the country without a visa or with one upon arrival, while others will need to apply ahead of time for one. To guarantee a seamless entry into the nation, it is crucial to confirm the particular criteria for your nationality well in advance of your trip.

Travelers should make sure their passport is valid for at least six months from the date of entry into Egypt in addition to obtaining a visa. A printed copy of your passport and visa should also be carried at all times, as you might need to show these documents to officials upon request.

2.3 Health and Safety Advice: Maintaining Your Health and Safety

Prioritizing your health and safety is essential when visiting Egypt. Even if the nation has a lot to offer in terms of historical and cultural attractions, it is still vital to take safety measures to keep oneself safe.

Staying hydrated is one of the most crucial health issues for visitors to Egypt, particularly in the sweltering summer months. To prevent sunburn, make sure you wear protective clothes and sunscreen, stay out of the sun, and drink lots of water.

Travelers should take care to prevent food and waterborne infections in addition to drinking plenty of water. Avoid eating raw or undercooked food, stick to bottled or filtered water, and use caution when eating street food or at restaurants with dubious sanitary standards.

Egypt is often regarded as a secure travel destination for travelers. But it's crucial to stay alert and conscious of your surroundings, particularly in busy tourist destinations and marketplaces where pickpocketing and small-time crime can happen.

Additionally, it is advised to travel with caution to some parts of Egypt, especially those close to the borders with Sudan and Libya, where there may be greater security threats. Check the most recent travel advisories issued by your government before departing for Egypt, and stay away from any regions that are considered dangerous.

2.4 Must-Pack Items: What to Bring

The climate, culture, and activities of Egypt must all be carefully taken into account when packing for a trip there. The following are some necessities to put on your packing list:

1. Lightweight, breathable clothing: To stay cool and comfortable in Egypt's hot weather, bring loose-fitting, lightweight clothing made of breathable materials like cotton or linen.

2. Sun protection: To shield yourself from the sun's harmful rays, pack lightweight clothing, sunglasses, a wide-brimmed hat, and sunscreen with a high SPF.

3. Comfortable walking shoes are essential whether you're strolling through busy bazaars or seeing ancient ruins.

4. Even though Egypt is a liberal nation, it is nonetheless polite to wear modestly, particularly when visiting places of worship. Make sure you bring clothes that conceal your cleavage, knees, and shoulders.

5. Bring a travel adapter if your gadgets require a different kind of plug

because Egypt utilizes the European-style two-pin plug.

6. Medication: Bring along any prescription drugs you may require, along with a basic first-aid kit filled with necessities like bandages, painkillers, and antidiarrheal medication.

7. Travel insurance: If you want to safeguard yourself against unforeseen circumstances like medical costs, cancelled trips, or misplaced luggage, think about getting travel insurance.

You can make sure you have a safe, pleasurable, and wonderful journey to Egypt, full of life-changing experiences and discoveries, by being prepared and following these crucial measures. Your trip to this enchanted land is sure to be an adventure of a lifetime, whether you're admiring the ancient grandeur of the pyramids, sailing the timeless waters of the Nile, or losing yourself in the colorful culture of modern Egypt.

3. GETTING TO EGYPT

Egypt invites visitors from all over the world to discover its historic wonders and dynamic culture because of its rich history and varied landscapes. It takes careful planning and awareness of the available transportation alternatives to get to and around this enchanted nation. We explore the different routes to Egypt in this comprehensive guide, as well as how to navigate its expansive terrain after you arrive.

3.1 Air Travel: Entry Point to the Pharaonic World

Egypt can be reached most easily and often by flight, with a number of international airports acting as Egypt's entry points. The majority of foreign passengers enter Egypt through Cairo International Airport, which is the busiest airport in the country and situated just outside the capital city of Cairo.

Egypt is served by other international airports in addition to Cairo, such as Luxor International Airport in Upper Egypt, Hurghada International Airport on the Red Sea coast, and Sharm El Sheikh International Airport in the Sinai Peninsula. These airports make it simple to travel to many parts of Egypt because they provide direct flights from major cities across the globe.

To get the greatest prices and availability, make sure to book your flights well in advance of your trip to Egypt. When planning your trip, take into account things like airline luggage rules, layovers, and departure times.

3.2 Traveling by Land: Seeing Egypt's Breathtaking Scenes

After you get to Egypt, you'll need to think about how to get around the huge and varied landscapes and attractions of the nation. Buses, railroads, taxis, and private automobile services are examples of land transportation options; each has pros and downsides of its own.

In Egypt, buses are a well-liked and reasonably priced mode of transportation between cities and towns; a number of private businesses run intercity bus services. These buses travel between popular tourist locations like Hurghada, Luxor, Aswan, Cairo, and Luxor. They are often clean and pleasant.

Another practical means of getting throughout Egypt's cities is via train, which provides pleasant seats and beautiful views of the surrounding area. Cairo is connected to locations around the nation via the vast passenger train network run by the Egyptian National Railways.

Major cities and popular tourist destinations have an abundance of taxis, making them an easy way to get around locally. Before beginning your trip, make sure to haggle over the fee with the driver and insist on utilizing the meter if one is available to prevent being overcharged.

If you're looking for more freedom and flexibility, renting a car can be a terrific way to visit Egypt's sights at your own speed. Egypt is home to a number of domestic and foreign automobile rental agencies offering anything from little cars to SUVs and luxury autos.

3.3 Using Public Transport to Get Around Egypt's Cities

Egypt has a range of options for moving around cities and towns in addition to intercity transit. Buses, trams, and the Cairo Metro—the first in Africa and the Arab world—are among the modes of public transit available in large cities like Cairo and Alexandria.

With two lines serving different parts of the city and future extension plans, the Cairo Metro is a quick, economical, and effective means to get around the capital. The metro is important for both locals and visitors because it runs from early in the morning until late at night.

Cairo offers a wide network of buses and minibuses that cover much of the city in addition to the metro. Although these buses can be busy and disorderly at times, they offer a moderately priced means of traveling to regions not covered by the metro.

The public transportation system in Alexandria, the second-biggest city in Egypt, consists of buses and trams that run routes that connect various neighborhoods and tourist destinations. In Cairo and Alexandria, there are also taxis and ride-hailing services like Uber and Careem, providing easy ways to move around the city.

3.4 Car Rental: Unrestricted Exploration

Travelers can easily see Egypt's sites at their own convenience and pace by hiring a car throughout the nation. Having your own car provides you the freedom to create your own schedule and drive wherever you like, whether you're thinking of taking a road trip down the Nile River, seeing the Western Desert, or driving to lonely ancient sites.

There are a few crucial points to bear in mind while leasing a car in Egypt. First and foremost, find a dependable rental car provider with an outstanding reputation for both car upkeep and customer service. Examine the rental agreement's terms and conditions, paying particular attention to the fuel limitations, mileage restrictions, and insurance coverage.

Learn about Egypt's traffic laws and regulations before you travel there, as they can be different from those in your native country. Particularly in cities, be ready for chaotic driving circumstances and drive carefully across busy crossroads and streets.

It's vital to always be vigilant and aware of your surroundings when driving in Egypt. Keep an eye out for other automobiles, cyclists, and pedestrians. You should also be ready for unforeseen difficulties like potholes, animals, and roadside vendors.

Renting a car in Egypt may be a fulfilling and unique way to discover the different landscapes and attractions of the nation, despite the difficulties associated. You can discover the marvels of this old region and have the independence and flexibility of owning your own vehicle with careful planning and preparation.

Extensive planning and research of the available transportation choices are important while traveling to and within Egypt. Egypt presents a number of alternatives for life-changing experiences and adventures, whether you're traveling independently by car rental, bus, or rail, or by plane into Cairo International Airport. You may make the most of your journey to this fascinating country of historical wonders and current marvels by selecting the modes of transportation that best fit your interests and manner of travel.

4. ACCOMODATIONS IN EGYPT

Any trip planning process must include selecting the appropriate place to stay, and Egypt has a vast array of housing possibilities to match any traveler's tastes and budget. Egypt provides a shelter for tourists looking for comfort, convenience, and authenticity, offering a variety of lodging options from lavish hotels and resorts to economical hostels and guesthouses, as well as unusual alternative lodging options. In this extensive guide, we evaluate the numerous kinds of housing that are offered in Egypt and highlight the distinctive experiences that each provide.

4.1 Resorts & Hotels: luxury and coziness

Egypt is home to a number of excellent hotels and resorts that offer luxurious accommodations, faultless service, and an abundance of amenities to meet any need or want. Egypt's hotels and resorts, which range from well-known buildings with breathtaking views of the Nile River to coastal resorts along the Red Sea coast, provide discerning travelers with a sanctuary of luxury and relaxation.

Luxurious lodgings in Cairo, such as the elegant Four Seasons Hotel Cairo at Nile Plaza and the storied Mena House Hotel, offer easy access to popular attractions like the Egyptian Museum and the Pyramids of Giza in addition to stunning skyline views.

Resorts can be located in Red Sea coastal towns including Hurghada,

Marsa Alam, and Sharm El Sheikh. These places provide sparkling waters, spotless beaches, and a range of recreational activities like water sports, diving, and snorkeling. Luxurious accommodations, fine dining, and unique amenities are offered by hotels such as the Ritz-Carlton, St. Regis, and Hilton, for those seeking the perfect beach vacation.

A tranquil sanctuary amidst the splendor of Egypt's archeological treasures may be found in hotels and resorts along the banks of the Nile River in the ancient city of Luxor. Resorts like the Hilton Luxor Resort & Spa and the Sofitel Winter Palace Luxor provide luxurious suites, verdant gardens, and stunning views of the Valley of the Kings and the Nile.

4.2 Hotels and Guesthouses: Budget-Friendly Accommodations

For travelers on a limited budget, Egypt offers a wide range of hostels and guesthouses that provide affordable accomodation without compromising on quality or convenience. Hostels are a popular choice for independent travelers and backpackers seeking inexpensive housing with shared utilities and the opportunity to meet other travelers from around the globe.

Well-known hostels in Cairo, such as the Australian Hostel Cairo and the Freedom Hostel, offer neat and comfortable dorm-style accommodations together with private rooms, communal kitchens, and facilities for guests to relax and socialize.

In Luxor, budget accommodations can be obtained near the city's core on the East Bank of the Nile at guesthouses and cheap hotels. The Luxor Museum and the Karnak Temple Complex, two of the city's main attractions, are easily accessible from these sites. Budget-conscious travelers will find affordable lodging options like the Bob Marley House Hostel and the Nefertiti Hotel Luxor, which offer warm staff, basic but comfortable rooms, and a relaxed atmosphere.

For those looking for cheap accommodation near popular diving spots and the beach, there are budget-friendly guesthouses and hostels along the Red Sea coast. Places like the Ocean View Hotel in Dahab and the Albatros Resort in Hurghada offer easy access to the area's vibrant nightlife and outdoor activities. These facilities likewise include helpful staff and basic yet adequate accommodations.

4.3 Substitute Facilities: Unique and Sincere Encounters

In addition to the standard hotels, resorts, and hostels, Egypt provides a wide selection of alternative housing options that offer unique and authentic experiences for travelers looking for something different from the ordinary. These alternative housing alternatives, which range from eco-friendly hotels and traditional guesthouses to desert camps and Nile River cruises, offer a glimpse into the rich culture, history, and scenic splendor of Egypt.

Known variously as "zawiyas" or "wakalas," traditional Egyptian guesthouses are an excellent means for tourists to experience a true sense of community and culture in Cairo and surrounding cities. Often located in historic neighborhoods, these guesthouses include traditional architecture, vintage furnishings, and personal care.

In Egypt's Western Desert, eco-lodges and desert camps provide a unique opportunity to experience the vast and pristine wildness of the country while minimising environmental impact. Resorts like the Bahariya Oasis's Desert Lodge and the Dakhla Oasis Eco-Lodge provide comfortable accommodations, locally produced food, and guided excursions of the area's natural treasures, historic ruins, and desert vistas.

Along the Nile River, luxurious cruise ships and traditional felucca sailboats offer a unique way to explore Egypt's ancient temples, monuments, and towns while enjoying the conveniences and comforts of onboard services and accommodations. Typically, Nile River cruises depart at Luxor and travel to Aswan, stopping at significant sites such as the Temple of Philae, the Valley of the Kings, and the Temple of Karnak.

5. CAIRO: AN ENTRANCE TO EGYPT'S RICH HISTORY AND CHANGING CULTURE

Cairo, the energetic capital of Egypt, is a city of contrasts, where innovation and tradition live in harmony with technology and the past. When it comes to internationally renowned institutions, iconic structures, thrilling entertainment, and delectable cuisine, Cairo has much to offer travelers who are eager to experience its lively atmosphere and extensive history. In this comprehensive guide, we examine the many attractions and cultural treasures that this flourishing city has to offer.

5.1 Landmarks and Attractions: Icons of Cairo's Past

Cairo is home to a large number of well-known landmarks and attractions that emphasize the city's cultural heritage and history. At the top of the list is the Giza Necropolis, which is home to the legendary Great Pyramid of Giza, the enigmatic Sphinx, and several ancient tombs and temples from the pharaonic period. Visiting this UNESCO World Heritage Site offers a glimpse into the once-unprecedently exquisite Egyptian ancient culture.

The Egyptian Museum, located nearby, has an abundance of antiquities and relics spanning thousands of years of Egyptian history. The museum's vast collection, which ranges from exquisite statues and sarcophagi to intricately crafted jewelry and royal mummies, depicts ancient Egyptian art, religion, and daily life.

Situated in the heart of Islamic Cairo, the historic Khan El-Khalili neighborhood beckons visitors with its mazy streets, bustling souks, and ornate mosques. Here, tourists may haggle for trinkets and handicrafts, take in architectural wonders like the Sultan Hassan Mosque and the Al-Azhar Mosque, and experience the sights, sounds, and scents of Cairo's vibrant street life.

For an aerial view of the city, a visit to the Cairo Tower is a must. Rising 187 meters above the banks of the Nile River, this well-known landmark offers breathtaking views of Cairo's skyline, including the historic Citadel of Saladin, the modern Zamalek and Heliopolis neighborhoods, and the Nile's meandering course as it flows through the city's center.

5.2 Museums and Galleries: Windows into Egypt's Cultural Heritage

In addition to the Egyptian Museum, Cairo is home to a diverse array of museums and galleries that honor Egypt's rich creative and cultural legacy. A remarkable collection of Islamic artifacts, including magnificent fabrics, illuminated manuscripts, and pottery, can be seen in the Museum of Islamic Art. It is kept in an exquisite 19th-century palace.

For lovers of modern art, the Palace of Arts and the Cairo Opera House offer a bustling cultural hub with exhibitions, performances, and events showcasing the creations of local and international artists. The Cairo Opera House, with its stunning modern building and cutting-edge facilities, shows opera, ballet, theater, and musical events all year long, while the Palace of Arts hosts rotating exhibitions of contemporary art, photography, and design.

The Coptic Museum provides a comprehensive overview of Egypt's ancient past by offering an engaging journey through the history of Egypt's Christian legacy, with relics and artworks spanning from the early Christian period to the Ottoman Empire. Highlights include historic manuscripts, sacred images, and architectural relics from Coptic churches and monasteries in Egypt.

5.3 Entertainment and Nightlife: Plenty and Variety

Cairo offers an as diverse range of entertainment alternatives as the city itself, encompassing everything from traditional folk music and dance to avant-garde theater, film, and nightlife. The El Sawy Culturewheel, a cultural center in Zamalek on the banks of the Nile, hosts a range of events and activities, including live music performances, film screenings, and art exhibitions.

To experience Cairo's dynamic street culture, head to the Downtown Cairo neighborhood, where bustling cafes, bars, and restaurants adorn the city's historic streets and squares. Here, you may mingle with locals, enjoy delicious Egyptian cuisine, and experience the lively atmosphere of this booming city.

Cairo boasts a vibrant nightlife scene that offers something for every taste and inclination throughout the evenings. From classic coffee shops and shisha lounges tucked away in the city's narrow passageways to rooftop pubs and nightclubs with views of the Nile, there are plenty of alternatives for an amazing night out on the town.

6. CULINARY DELIGHTS

Egyptian cuisine is a delectable fusion of tastes and influences that captures the country's diversity in geography and culture. Cairo offers a culinary experience that is unmatched, from hearty street food that is filled with aromatic spices to sumptuous dinners fit for a king.

A substantial dish consisting of rice, lentils, pasta, and chickpeas, topped with crispy fried onions and a sharp tomato sauce, is known as koshary. You should also try ful medames, a hearty stew of fava beans eaten with bread and pickled vegetables, and taameya, an Egyptian version of falafel prepared with ground fava beans and seasonings.

To sample some of Cairo's vibrant street food culture, visit bustling markets like Khan El-Khalili and Midan Hussein. Here, vendors provide a mouthwatering assortment of sweets and snacks, such as desserts, freshly baked pastries, and grilled meats and kebabs.

For the more discerning diner, Cairo offers a wide range of eateries serving anything from international cuisine to traditional Egyptian dishes. The Egyptian capital offers an abundance of options for an excellent eating experience, from sophisticated rooftop eateries overlooking the Nile to modern cafes and bistros in trendy areas like Maadi and Zamalek.

Cairo is a city where the past and current coexist together and is full of surprises and delights. Cairo provides a wide range of activities for tourists eager to explore its vibrant atmosphere and rich history, from world-renowned landmarks and first-rate museums to thrilling entertainment venues and delectable cuisine. Whether they are marveling at the pyramids, haggling over souvenirs in the souks, or savoring the flavors of Egyptian food, visitors to Cairo are sure to leave an impact.

7. DISCOVERING ANCIENT SITES: EGYPT'S EVERLASTING MYSTERIES

Egypt is a mythological and ancient history-rich nation with many riches found in its historic sites that have drawn travelers for years. The iconic Pyramids of Giza, the exquisite Luxor temples, the mysterious Abu Simbel ruins, and other historic sites in Egypt offer a glimpse into the grandeur and splendor of a civilization that existed thousands of years ago. We'll take a time travel tour to explore some of Egypt's most well-known historical sites and understand more about its fascinating past with the aid of this comprehensive guide.

7.1 Giza Pyramids: Icons of Ancient Egypt

Any vacation to Egypt must include a view of the magnificent Pyramids of Giza, one of the Seven Wonders of the Ancient World and possibly the most famous ancient structure on the planet. The three main pyramids at the Giza Necropolis, which is located outside of Cairo, are the Great Pyramid of Khufu, the Pyramid of Khafre, and the Pyramid of Menkaure. Along with the enigmatic Sphinx and several smaller pyramids, there are also numerous smaller satellite tombs and pyramids.

Built over 4,500 years ago as magnificent tombs for the pharaohs, the pyramids are a testament to the technical prowess and imagination of the ancient Egyptians. The largest and most well-known of the three is the Great Pyramid of Khufu, standing a staggering 146 meters (481 feet) high.

It was the highest man-made edifice on Earth for almost 3,800 years.

Visitors to the Giza Pyramids can explore the intricate passageways, rooms, and burial chambers hidden beneath the intimidating exteriors of the pyramids. An interesting glimpse into the ideas of the ancient Egyptians regarding the afterlife may be found in the nearby Solar Boat Museum, which exhibits a restored solar boat that was buried close to the Great Pyramid for Khufu's journey to the afterlife.

7.2 Luxor and the Valley of the Kings: Temples and Tombs of the Pharaohs

Luxor, on the banks of the Nile River in Upper Egypt, is often called the "world's greatest open-air museum" because of its profusion of historical buildings and archaeological monuments. Located in the heart of Luxor lies the spectacular Temple of Karnak, a vast complex of temples, chapels, and obelisks dedicated to the god Amun-Ra. Built over 2,000 years, Karnak is a masterpiece of ancient Egyptian architecture. It also reminds us of the pharaohs' strong religious beliefs.

Situated across the Nile from Karnak, the similarly spectacular Temple of Luxor was built by Amenhotep III and then enlarged by Ramses II. Towering columns, enormous statues, and finely carved reliefs depicting scenes from ancient Egyptian mythology and history can all be found within this spectacular temple complex.

The Valley of the Kings, outside of Luxor, is a UNESCO World Heritage Site where the pharaohs and nobles of the New Kingdom were interred. Explore the elaborate tombs of kings such as Seti I, Ramses II, and Tutankhamun. The vibrantly painted paintings and hieroglyphic inscriptions adorning the tombs shed light on the ideas the ancient Egyptians held toward the afterlife.

7.3 Aswan and Abu Simbel: Temples Along the Nile Coastal Plain

Situated further south along the Nile is the city of Aswan, renowned for its immense natural beauty and rich archaeological past. Aswan's core is home to the Temple of Philae, dedicated to the goddess Isis. After the construction of the Aswan High Dam, it was relocated to Agilkia Island. The temple features sanctuaries, colonnades, and beautifully preserved reliefs that shed light on ancient Egyptian religious practices.

The temples of Abu Simbel are among the most well-known and impressive buildings in Egypt. They're not far from Aswan. Built by Ramses II in the thirteenth century BCE, the Great Temple of Abu Simbel honors the gods Amun-Ra, Ra-Horakhty, and Ptah. The smaller Temple of Hathor honors Queen Nefertari, the beloved wife of Ramses II. Among the most famous aspects of the temples are their large sculptures, intricate carvings, and the twice-yearly "Sun Festival," which takes place when the sun aligns with the sanctuary to illuminate the inner sanctum.

7.4 Assembled Artifacts from Hellenistic and Roman Egypt around the Mediterranean Coast and Alexandria

Alexandria, a historic city on Egypt's Mediterranean coast that was once regarded as one of the greatest cities in antiquity, was founded by Alexander the Great in the fourth century BCE. Though much has been lost to the passage of time, there are still many noteworthy landmarks and archaeological sites in ancient Alexandria. These include the Bibliotheca Alexandrina, a modern library and cultural center that pays homage to the historic Library of Alexandria, the Roman Amphitheater, and the Kom el Shoqafa Catacombs.

The submerged remains of the ancient city of Heracleion at Abu Qir Bay, which lies close by, offer an intriguing glimpse into the world of Hellenistic Egypt. Heracleion was discovered in the early 20th century and is believed to have had a major role in Ptolemaic and Roman history as a port city and center of religion.

8. A JOURNEY ALONG THE NILE: A CRUISE THROUGH EGYPT'S HEARTLAND

Exploring Egypt's history and heartland while cruising down the Nile, the world's longest river, is an enduring trip. From the bustling streets of Cairo to the placid waters of Lake Nasser, Nile River cruises offer a unique perspective on Egypt's breathtaking natural beauty, ancient monuments, and intricate cultural legacy. In this comprehensive guide, we explore the allure of Nile River cruises and showcase some of the main sights along this legendary river.

8.1 Nile River Cruise: The Ultimate Egyptian Experience

Nile River cruises appeal to tourists who wish to see Egypt's contemporary and historical riches while indulging in the luxuries of a floating hotel. Typically, Nile cruises travel from Luxor to Aswan, making stops along the way at significant historical landmarks and popular tourist spots.

Most Nile cruises span three to seven nights, which allows passengers ample time to gradually take in the Nile Valley's natural splendor. From lavish five-star ships with spacious bedrooms, gourmet dining, and onboard amenities like spas and swimming pools to more affordable dahabiyyas—ancient sailing boats that offer a more intimate and authentic experience—the ships themselves vary in size.

One of the delights of Nile River cruises is witnessing the timeless landscape and traditional communities that line the riverbanks. While the ship gently glides over the river, passengers can relax on deck and take in the sights and sounds of daily life along the Nile, from fishermen to farmers tending to their nets.

8.2 Attractions Along the Nile: Temples, Villages, and Historic Tombs

Along the Nile River are several ancient temples, tombs, and monuments that offer insight into Egypt's rich past and cultural legacy. Guests on Nile River cruises can explore some of the most well-known and preserved archaeological sites in the world, such as:

The Valley of the Kings, where visitors can tour the elaborate tombs of pharaohs including Seti I, Ramses II, and Tutankhamun, and the Temple of Karnak and Luxor are highlights of Luxor, which is known as the "world's greatest open-air museum."

- Edfu: On the west bank of the Nile, Edfu is home to the Temple of Horus, one of Egypt's best-preserved ancient temples. The temple, which honors the falcon-headed god Horus, features stunning entrance pylon views over the surrounding countryside, intricate reliefs, and massive columns.

- Kom Ombo: Perched on a picturesque bend in the Nile, the peculiar Temple of Kom Ombo honors the gods Sobek and Horus. The temple is known for its twofold structure, with two sanctuaries and parallel colonnades that shed light on ancient Egyptian religious practices.

Aswan: Often called the "Jewel of the Nile," Aswan is a quaint city nestled along the banks of the river. The Temple of Philae, the Unfinished Obelisk, and the Nubian colonies of Elephantine Island are just a few of the many sites that can be seen here. In addition, travelers have the option of taking additional trips from Aswan to the enigmatic Abu Simbel temples, which are located close to Lake Nasser.

- Nile Villages: Guests on Nile River cruises have the opportunity to explore the ancient cities and villages that have long been a part of the Nile Valley. From the colorful marketplaces of Esna and the pottery studios of Fustat to the verdant fields of the Nile Delta, these towns offer a glimpse into the timeless rhythms of rural life in Egypt.

Travelers can enjoy a variety of onboard facilities and activities in addition to exploring historical monuments and other locations during Nile River cruises. With cultural discussions, cooking demonstrations, live entertainment, and traditional music and dance performances, a Nile cruise never has a dull moment.

9. TRAVEL ITINERARIES

Egypt is a gateway to a world of breathtaking scenery, vibrant civilizations, and historical wonders. With so many locations to choose from and a history spanning thousands of years, planning a trip can be both exhilarating and daunting. Whether you have a week, two weeks, or even a month to spend visiting Egypt, this book will help you make the most of your trip with detailed travel itineraries tailored to different time frames.

9.1 One-Week Schedule: Highlights of Egypt

For travelers with limited time, a one-week itinerary offers a concise synopsis of Egypt's most well-known locations and must-see attractions. With this itinerary, you may experience a well-balanced blend of history, culture, and adventure while seeing the finest of Egypt in just seven days.

Days 1-2: Cairo

- Begin your journey in Cairo, the bustling capital of Egypt. Visit the Sphinx and the Great Pyramid of Khufu, two of the most well-known Pyramids of Giza, and explore the ancient Saqqara necropolis.
- Spend the afternoon exploring the Egyptian Museum, which houses a sizable collection of artifacts, including Tutankhamun's wealth.

Enjoy the sights, sounds, and fragrances of Khan El-Khalili, Cairo's well-known bazaar, as you meander through its vibrant streets at night.

Days 3–4: Luxor

Consider Luxor the "World's Greatest Open-Air Museum." Fly or take an overnight train there and visit the Karnak Temple Complex, Luxor Temple, and the Avenue of Sphinxes.

- Visit the Valley of the Kings, the Valley of the Queens, and the Hatshepsut Mortuary Temple located on the west bank of the Nile.
- Take a leisurely stroll down the Nile Corniche in the evening to see the sunset over the river.

Days 4-5: Aswan

- Travel to Aswan, which is known for its breathtaking scenery and Nubian culture, in the south. Travel by boat to the picturesque Agilkia Island, where you can see the majestic Philae Temple, dedicated to the goddess Isis.
- Discover the regional customs and traditions by visiting the Nubian villages on the west bank of the Nile. You can also take advantage of the friendly hospitality of the Nubian people.
- Take a felucca ride down the Nile, passing Elephantine Island and the Aga Khan Mausoleum.

Day 7: Departure

- On your last day in Egypt, take a tour of Aswan's vibrant marketplaces. Souvenirs, spices, and handicrafts can all be purchased here.
- Depending on when your flight is departing, you might have time to visit the Nubian Museum or take one last stroll down the Corniche before you head to the airport.

9.2 Two Week Timetable: All-Inclusive Egypt Tour

If you have two weeks to spare, you can discover hidden pearls and less-frequented sites while delving deeper into Egypt's treasures. This itinerary allows us a more leisurely pace, with time to see Cairo, Luxor, Aswan, and other lesser-known destinations.

Days 1-4 in Cairo

- Spend the first four days in Cairo, allowing time to see the Giza Pyramids, the Egyptian Museum, and the Khan El-Khalili bazaar, among other notable locations.
- Take a day trip to nearby locations, such as Memphis' ancient city, the Step Pyramid of Djoser at Saqqara, and the remains of Heliopolis, the ancient capital.

Days 5–8: Nile Cruise from Luxor to Aswan

- Take a four-day Nile cruise departing Luxor for Aswan, stopping along the way at important sites. Highlights of the trip include visits to the temples of Kom Ombo, Luxor, Edfu, and Karnak as well as trips to the west bank of the Nile to view the Temple of Hatshepsut, the Valley of the Kings, and the Valley of the Queens.

Days 9–12: Aswan and Abu Simbel

- After disembarking from the cruise, spend the next four days exploring Aswan and the surrounding areas. See the Philae Temple, the High Dam, and the Unfinished Obelisk by taking a boat excursion to the Nubian settlements on the western bank of the Nile.

- Take a day trip to Abu Simbel, the location of the magnificent temples of Ramses II and Nefertari, which were shifted to a higher altitude during the construction of the Aswan High Dam in order to prevent floods.

Days 13–14 in Alexandria

Explore Alexandria, the country's second-largest metropolis and a historical and cultural treasure trove. See the Catacombs of Kom El Shoqafa, the Bibliotheca Alexandrina, and the Citadel of Qaitbay. Visit the city's charming neighborhoods, waterfront promenades, and souks as well.

- Spend your final day in Alexandria relaxing on the gorgeous beaches, dining at local restaurants that specialize in seafood, and soaking up the Mediterranean environment before returning to Cairo to bid adieu.

9.3 Monthly Program: Comprehensive Tour of Egypt

Travelers with the luxury of time can get a close-up view of Egypt's diverse landscapes, intriguing history, and vibrant culture by planning a one-month itinerary. This itinerary covers both the major sights and lesser-known spots in Egypt, providing a comprehensive picture of everything the country has to offer.

Days 1-6: Cairo and Giza

- After arriving in Cairo, spend the first week of your vacation exploring the city's top attractions, including the Giza Pyramids, the Egyptian Museum, and the Khan El-Khalili bazaar.

- Take day visits to nearby cities like Saqqara, Memphis, and Heliopolis. -

Visit the historic districts of Islamic Cairo, such as the Khanqah of Sultan Baybars, the Citadel, and the Al-Azhar Mosque.

Luxor to Aswan Nile Cruise: Days 8–14

- Take a seven-day Nile cruise departing Luxor for Aswan, stopping along the way at important sites. Highlights of the trip include visits to the temples of Kom Ombo, Luxor, Edfu, and Karnak as well as trips to the west bank of the Nile to view the Temple of Hatshepsut, the Valley of the Kings, and the Valley of the Queens.

Days 15–21: Aswan, Abu Simbel, and the Western Desert

After disembarking from the cruise, spend the following seven days exploring Aswan and the surrounding areas. See the Philae Temple, the High Dam, and the Unfinished Obelisk by taking a boat excursion to the Nubian settlements on the western bank of the Nile.

- Take a day trip to Abu Simbel, the location of the magnificent temples of Ramses II and Nefertari, and visit the nearby temples of Wadi El Seboua and Amada.

Spend a few days exploring the Western Desert, including the White and Black Deserts and the oasis areas of Siwa, Bahariya, and Farafra. Sand dunes, salt flats, hot springs, and ancient rock formations are some of the attractions of the Western Desert.

Days 22–28: Red Sea Coast and

Sinai Peninsula

- Visit the Red Sea resort town of Hurghada, where you can relax on the beach, take a dip or snorkel in the crystal-clear waters, and visit nearby attractions like Giftun Island and the Hurghada Marina.
- Visit the Sinai Peninsula, where you may hike Mount Sinai to see the sunrise, explore the seaside town of Dahab, and see the Monastery of St. Catherine.

Days 29–30: Alexandria travel

- Travel to Alexandria, where you will spend the final few days exploring the ancient sites, including the Bibliotheca Alexandrina, the Catacombs of Kom El Shoqafa, and the Citadel of Qaitbay.
- Depending on when you're departing from Cairo International Airport, you could have time for one more stroll along Alexandria's breathtaking beaches or a visit to a local seafood restaurant.

Make the most of your time in Egypt by planning your itinerary, whether you have a week, two weeks, or a month to spend discovering this intriguing nation. Egypt offers a wide range of experiences that are just waiting to be explored, from historic sites and ancient wonders to natural landscapes and cultural gems. By following these detailed itineraries, you may enjoy a trip of a lifetime to Egypt, learning about its rich past and experiencing its dynamic present. So prepare for a thrilling journey, pack your possessions, and embark on your dream journey over the land of the pharaohs. Egypt's boundless beauty and ageless pleasures are waiting to astound, inspire, and enthrall you.

10. ARID JOURNEYS: EXPLORING EGYPT'S ENIGMATIZED LANDSCAPES

The mysterious nature of Egypt's deserts has long piqued the curiosity of travelers and explorers. For those seeking exploration and adventure, these vast expanses of sand and rock—which span from the wild terrain of the Sinai Peninsula to the remote oases of the Western Desert—are a playground. In this comprehensive book, we delve into the several exciting experiences that tourists can have in Egypt's deserts, ranging from exploring historic oases to embarking on thrilling safari trips.

10.1 Western Desert Oases: Dry terrain encircling paradise towns

The vast desert region of Egypt, referred to as the Western Desert, stretches from the Nile Valley to the Libyan border. Despite its severe and inhospitable temperature, the desert is home to a variety of oases, which are lush pockets of life and civilization amidst the barren surrounds. Among these oasis, the most well-known ones are:

- Siwa Oasis: Known for its remarkable natural beauty and unique cultural history, Siwa Oasis is one of Egypt's most remote and picturesque oases. It is located near the Libyan border. Surrounded by towering sand dunes and lush palm groves, Siwa is home to ancient ruins, hot springs, and the legendary Temple of the Oracle, which is thought to have served as

Alexander the Great's meeting spot when he sought divine guidance.

Bahariya Oasis: Tucked away in the heart of the Western Desert, Bahariya Oasis is a fruitful agricultural region known for its date palms, olive trees, and mineral-rich hot springs. The oasis may contain a number of historic locations, including the Valley of the Golden Mummies, which is home to hundreds of discovered Greco-Roman mummies.

A little further south, Dakhla Oasis is a tranquil oasis surrounded by ancient caravan routes and sand dunes. The oasis, with its ancient mosques, mud-brick homes, and Roman ruins, offers a glimpse into the rich history and culture of Egypt's desert communities.

- Kharga Oasis: Known for its olive trees, date palms, and citrus orchards, Kharga Oasis is a thriving agricultural area in the Western Desert and one of Egypt's most populous and largest oases. The oasis is home to a plethora of historical buildings, including the Temple of Hibis, an ancient Egyptian temple dedicated to the god Amun.

Discovering the Western Desert oasis allows visitors to immerse themselves in the timeless rhythms of the desert, such as strolling through historic ruins, soaking in natural hot springs beneath a starry desert sky, and sipping tea in a traditional mud-brick cafe.

Sinai Peninsula: Enchantment and Nature

The Sinai Peninsula is a rugged, mountainous region that is noted for its historical significance and stunning natural beauty. It is nestled between the

Mediterranean and Red Seas. Enjoy a wide range of outdoor activities and cultural experiences in Sinai, from the stunning beaches of Dahab and Sharm El Sheikh to the towering peaks of Mount Sinai, catering to visitors of all ages and interests.

- Mount Sinai: Rising to a height of 2,285 meters (7,497 feet), Mount Sinai is the highest point in the Sinai Peninsula and a highly revered pilgrimage site for Christians, Muslims, and Jews. Travelers can see the surrounding desert at dawn or dusk by ascending to the mountain's summit. Most famously, the mountain is thought to be the place where Moses is supposed to have received the Ten Commandments.

- Saint Catherine's Monastery: Located at the foot of Mount Sinai, Saint Catherine's Monastery is one of the oldest Christian monasteries in the world and a UNESCO World Heritage Site. Established in the sixth century by the Byzantine Emperor Justinian I, the monastery has a priceless collection of religious artifacts, manuscripts, and icons, as well as the Burning Bush, said to be the site of God's appearance to Moses.

- Dahab and Sharm El Sheikh: Popular beach communities on the Red Sea coast, these areas are well-known for their excellent diving and snorkeling sites, immaculate waters, and vibrant coral reefs. There are plenty of opportunities for adventure and leisure in Dahab and Sharm El Sheikh, from exploring colorful coral gardens and underwater caves to relaxing on sun-kissed beaches and indulging in delicious seafood at beachside restaurants.

Excitement and thrills based on the sand with Desert Safari Tours

For those seeking a more daring adventure in Egypt's deserts, desert safari vacations are the perfect opportunity to explore the dry landscapes and hidden treasures of the Sahara. From exhilarating off-road drives across sand dunes to stargazing beneath the stars in a Bedouin-style desert camp, desert safari tours provide an amazing adventure into the heart of the desert.

White Desert: Located in the heart of the Western Desert, the White Desert is renowned for its bizarre landscape of chalk-white rock formations molded by wind and sand erosion. Sandboarding, camel riding, and stargazing in the open desert are common activities offered by desert safari excursions to the White Desert, in addition to seeing well-known locations like the Mushroom Rock, Crystal Mountain, and the Valley of the Whales.

- Black Desert: The name of this neighboring location comes from the stark contrast between the surrounding golden sands and the dark volcanic rock formations. Go on a desert safari adventure through the Black Desert and discover ancient lava flows, extinct volcanic cones, and hidden oasis. Meet the local Bedouin tribes and learn about their customs.

- Great Sand Sea: Stretching over the border between Egypt and Libya, the Great Sand Sea is one of the biggest sand dune deserts in the world. Its enormous dunes can grow as high as 140 meters (460 ft). On desert safari excursions to the Great Sand Sea, exciting activities like dune bashing, sandboarding, and quad biking are offered. In the middle of a desert, you can also sleep under the stars.

To sum up, desert tours provide travelers the opportunity to see some of Egypt's most remote and stunning landscapes, from the rugged Sinai Peninsula highlands to the verdant Western Desert oases. Adventurers and explorers of all stripes can have an array of life-altering experiences in Egypt's deserts, whether they opt to walk to the summit of Mount Sinai, go on a safari tour through the sand dunes, or scuba dive into the Red Sea's immaculate waters.

10.2 Underwater Wonders: Exploring the Underwater World

Thanks to its clear waters, vibrant coral reefs, and an abundance of marine life, the Red Sea is among the best places in the world to go diving. The Red Sea attracts scuba divers and snorkelers from around the globe due to its comfortable temperatures, exceptional transparency, and diverse underwater landscape. This comprehensive book dives into the lure of diving in the Red Sea, including the greatest resorts, places to dive and snorkel, and the variety of marine life that makes its depths home.

Red Sea Resorts: The Portal to an Underwater Paradise

A lot of the Red Sea's coastline resorts are great places to start diving and snorkeling trips. These resorts offer a range of accommodation choices, from luxurious beachfront hotels to reasonably priced guesthouses, as well as convenient access to the top dive sites and marine attractions in the region. Some of the most popular Red Sea destinations for divers and snorkelers are listed below:

- Sharm El Sheikh: One of Egypt's most sought-after diving destinations, Sharm El Sheikh is renowned for its vibrant coral reefs, glistening waters, and a profusion of marine life. It is located on the Sinai Peninsula's southernmost point. The resort town provides a range of dive facilities, hotels, and services to suit divers of all skill levels, as well as convenient access to popular dive destinations like Ras Mohammed National Park, Tiran Island, and the Straits of Tiran.

- Hurghada: Another popular diving destination, Hurghada offers a wide range of dive sites and marine attractions. It is situated on the mainland of Egypt. The resort town offers a range of accommodation, food, and entertainment options, as well as easy access to dive destinations such Giftun Island, Abu Nuhas Reef, and the Thistlegorm wreck.

- Marsa Alam: Further south along the Red Sea coast, Marsa Alam is a more tranquil and remote diving site, known for its pristine reefs, pristine coral gardens, and plenty of marine life. The resort town offers handy access to dive sites like as Elphinstone Reef, Abu Dabbab, and the Marsa Mubarak Marine Park, and a range of housing alternatives including opulent beach resorts and eco-friendly lodges.

Submerged Eden: Locations for Snorkeling and Diving

The Red Sea offers a wide variety of dive sites and locations that appeal to divers and snorkelers of all experience levels. Numerous opportunities for exploration and discovery are presented by the Red Sea's diverse underwater ecosystems, which include colorful coral reefs, eye-catching drop-offs, underwater tunnels, and wrecks. Some of the top locations in the Red Sea for snorkeling and diving are:

Ras Mohammed National Park: One of the most popular diving destinations in the Red Sea, Ras Mohammed is renowned for its amazing coral reefs, abundance of marine life, and magnificent underwater views. It is located close to the Sinai Peninsula's southernmost point. Highlights include Shark Reef, where divers can view schools of barracuda, jackfish, and reef sharks, and Yolanda Reef, which is home to colorful coral gardens and the remnants of the Yolanda cargo ship.

- Brothers Islands: Located in the middle of the Red Sea, the Brothers Islands are two remote, uninhabited islands renowned for their pristine reefs, towering walls, and plethora of aquatic life. The islands provide some of the most challenging and thrilling Red Sea diving, with opportunities to dive the Aida II and Numidia wrecks and observe pelagic species like whale, thresher, and hammerhead sharks.

- Elphinstone Reef: Elphinstone Reef, which is near Marsa Alam, is a well-known diving site that draws large pelagic species because of its strong currents, sheer walls, and encounters. The reef is home to a vast range of marine creatures, including schooling hammerhead sharks, oceanic whitetip sharks, and manta rays, in addition to vivid coral gardens and underwater caverns.

- Abu Dabbab: Adjacent to Marsa Alam, this small, protected bay offers excellent snorkeling for families and novices. There are vibrant coral gardens full of life to be seen, as well as vibrant reef fish, green sea turtles, and local dugongs, also referred to as sea cows.

10.3 Marine Life: A Diver's Paradise

The Red Sea is home to an astounding array of marine life, including pelagic species, enigmatic deep-diving giants, vivid reef fish, and coral gardens. When diving and snorkeling the waters of the Red Sea, one may see a variety of aquatic species, such as:

Coral Reefs: The Red Sea is renowned for its vibrant coral reefs, which are home to a broad range of hard and soft corals, including brain, table, and branching corals. Crustaceans, invertebrates, and colorful reef fish are just a few of the aquatic life that live in and feed off of these coral reefs.

- Fish: The Red Sea is home to about 1,200 distinct kinds of fish, ranging in size from tiny reef dwellers to large pelagic species. Larger predators like barracuda, tuna, and trevally are often spotted, along with smaller fish like butterflyfish, angelfish, parrotfish, and clownfish. Divers may also infrequently see oceanic whitetip and hammerhead sharks in addition to reef sharks like blacktip and whitetip.

- Turtles: The Red Sea serves as an essential breeding and feeding habitat for a number of sea turtle species, including loggerhead, green, and hawksbill turtles. Snorkelers and divers exploring the Red Sea's reefs may spot these graceful creatures munching on sea grass beds or relaxing on rocky ledges.

- Sharks: The Red Sea is home to a variety of shark species, including grey, blacktip, and whitetip reef sharks. Shark encounters are rare, but divers who search offshore and remote dive sites can be lucky enough to witness these amazing predators in their natural habitat.

In conclusion, diving in the Red Sea offers an incredible, once-in-a-lifetime opportunity to explore a world of vibrant coral reefs, an abundance of marine life, and stunning underwater landscape. Discover the many opportunities for exploration and discovery that the Red Sea's diverse and pristine underwater ecosystems present, whether you're diving with sharks in the Brothers Islands, snorkeling with sea turtles at Abu Dabbab, or exploring the colorful reefs of Ras Mohammed. The Red Sea's warm waters, excellent visibility, and top-notch dive sites make it a diver's dream come true.

11. DISCOVERING EGYPT'S DIVERSE CULTURAL LEGACY THROUGH IMMERSIONS

Travelers from all over the world are captivated by Egypt's unique mosaic culture, which is woven from centuries of history, customs, and many influences. Egypt offers a plethora of opportunities for visitors to interact with its dynamic indigenous populations and abundant cultural legacy; these include authentic homestays, cultural immersion programs, and traditional festivals and bustling markets. In this book, we delve into the cultural experiences that travelers can have in Egypt, including traditional festivals and celebrations, local markets and bazaars, and the eye-opening advantages of homestays and cultural immersion.

11.1 Traditional Festivals and Celebrations: Paying Tributaries to History and Custom

Egypt's calendar is full of customary holidays and festivities that pay tribute to the country's rich religious and cultural history. Bright religious celebrations and colorful folk festivals offer visitors a unique opportunity to fully experience Egyptian culture.

- Eid al-Fitr: One of the most important religious holidays in Islam, Eid al-Fitr marks the completion of Ramadan, the Islamic holy month of fasting. To commemorate Eid al-Fitr, Muslims gather with their loved ones and engage in feasting, prayer, and charitable giving. The occasion is a time of joy and celebration, with the streets decorated with bright decorations and traditional foods like baklava and ma'amoul.

- Sham el-Nessim: This Pharaonic-era celebration of "smelling the breeze" is an old Egyptian tradition. The Monday following Coptic Easter is Sham el-Nessim, a holiday that marks the arrival of spring and the beginning of farming season. Families gather in gardens and parks for picnics, enjoying traditional fare like as salted fish and feseekh, a fermented fish dish.

Moulid Festivals: Also referred to as awliya, these religious celebrations honor Muslim saints and Sufi mystics. These festivities feature processions, music, dance, and storytelling in addition to food stalls and market vendors selling traditional treats, candies, and handicrafts. The most famous Moulid festival in Egypt is the Moulid of Sayyidna al-Hussein, which is held in the old part of Islamic Cairo.

- Coptic Christmas: On January 7th, the Coptic Christian community in Egypt observes Coptic Christmas. The event includes church services, processions, traditional rites, and happy get-togethers with loved ones. Visitors can experience a bit of the rich cultural traditions of Coptic Christmas by taking part in the celebrations in Coptic districts such as Old Cairo and Maadi, as well as by attending church services.

11.2 Local Markets and Bazaars: Exploring Egypt's Changing Souks

Egypt's souks, also known as markets and bazaars, are bustling hubs of activity where locals and visitors alike go to shop, socialize, and savor the diverse range of the country's food. Egypt's souks, which range from ancient, historically significant souks to modern, vibrant marketplaces, are a visual feast for the senses.

Khan El-Khalili: Located in the heart of Islamic Cairo, Khan El-Khalili is one of Egypt's most renowned and historic souks, having been around since the 14th century. The narrow alleyways and meandering streets of Khan El-Khalili are packed with merchants selling an incredible array of goods, from souvenirs and jewelry to spices, textiles, and antiquities. Visitors can sip tea in traditional cafes, haggle with vendors, and take in the sights, sounds, and fragrances of this old marketplace.

- Aswan Souk: A glimpse into Nubian culture and tradition may be had in this vibrant and bustling market. It's situated along the Nile River's banks. The market is well-known for its bright scarves, ceramics, baskets, and other traditional Nubian wares in addition to textiles and handicrafts. Apart from browsing the kiosks and chatting with the local artisans, tourists can purchase unique keepsakes to reminisce about their trip to Aswan.

- Luxor Souk: Adjacent to the historic Temple of Luxor, Luxor Souk is a bustling marketplace where visitors may buy spices, perfumes, textiles, and souvenirs. Both locals and tourists love hanging out at the market because of its wide assortment of affordably priced goods. In addition to dining locally and strolling around the market's winding alleys, visitors may take in the vibrant ambiance of this busy marketplace.

11.3 Homestays and Cultural Immersion: Creating Connections with Local Communities

Through homestays and cultural immersion programs, tourists seeking a more authentic and in-depth cultural experience can meet people, learn about customs and traditions, and gain an intimate glimpse into Egyptian daily life.

- Nubian Homestays: In Aswan and other southern Egyptian locations, guests can stay with Nubian families in their customary mud-brick dwellings, known as Nubian villages. Through Nubian homestays, you may get a taste of the warmth, cuisine, and customs of the Nubian people. Additionally, you can participate in music and dance performances, boat cruises on the Nile, and culinary courses.

- Bedouin Camps: Guests can spend time in Bedouin camps to experience firsthand the nomadic lifestyle of Egypt's desert regions, including the Sinai Peninsula. Apart from offering basic accommodation in traditional tents or huts, Bedouin camps also provide opportunities for camel trekking, stargazing under the desert sky, and safaris. The timeless rhythms of the desert may be felt, meals can be shared with hosts, and Bedouin customs and traditions can be learned by guests.

- Cultural Exchange Programs: Various organizations and travel agencies provide cultural exchange programs that enable guests to become familiar with Egyptian customs and culture, engage in community service, and learn about Egyptian society. These programs present a unique opportunity to make a positive impact while learning more about Egypt's rich cultural heritage and social issues.

In conclusion, there are a plethora of cultural experiences accessible in Egypt for tourists who want to thoroughly immerse themselves in the country's rich history and vibrant local communities. Egypt's cultural riches present innumerable opportunities for travel, learning, and engagement with the people and traditions that define this unique country. These options include everything from authentic homestays and cultural immersion programs to bustling marketplaces and traditional festivals. Whether it's attending a Moulid celebration in Cairo, haggling over treasures in Aswan's souk, or eating dinner with a Nubian family in their house, visitors visiting Egypt are sure to leave with enduring cultural memories.

12. HELPFUL ADVICE FOR TRAVELERS TO EGYPT

Egypt is an intriguing travel destination with a vibrant culture, a rich history, and stunning natural surroundings. However, overcoming common challenges like currency translation, tipping customs, language barriers, and cultural etiquette can significantly impact how pleasurable a vacation is. In this book, we'll cover essential practical information for travelers visiting Egypt, including money and banking, language and communication, tipping etiquette, and regional customs and manners.

12.1 Currency and Banking: Understanding Egyptian Monetary Concerns

Egypt's national currency is the Egyptian Pound (EGP), or "livre égyptienne" in French. LE is a common acronym for it. Lesser units of measurement, like piastres, are equal to one Egyptian pound.

- Currency Exchange: Services for exchanging currencies are offered by banks, exchange offices, and hotels. It is advisable to exchange money at banks or official currency bureaus to ensure a fair exchange rate. When converting money, stay away from unofficial money changers and street sellers as they may provide poor rates or counterfeit currency.

- ATMs and Credit Cards: Travelers can withdraw Egyptian Pounds from ATMs, which are extensively dispersed throughout major cities and well-liked tourist spots, using international debit or credit cards. Visa and

MasterCard are widely accepted at hotels, restaurants, and retail stores, especially in popular tourist locations. It is a good idea to carry some cash on hand for smaller purchases and in more remote areas where credit card acceptance may be restricted.

- Traveler's Checks: Traveler's checks are no longer commonly recognized in Egypt, despite the fact that they were once a popular way for visitors to exchange money. It is advisable to carry both cash and debit/credit cards for convenience and flexibility.

12.2 Language and Communication: Overcoming Barriers

Arabic is the official language of Egypt; Modern Standard Arabic is used in formal settings and in the media. However, the Arabic dialect known as "Amiyya," which is Egyptian, is more frequently utilized in informal talks and day-to-day interactions.

English: English is widely spoken and understood, particularly at tourist destinations, lodging facilities, dining establishments, and retail stores. For English-speaking visitors, interacting with tour guides, hotel staff, and taxi drivers in tourist areas is quite simple, as the majority of them know basic English.

Basic Arabic words: While not necessary, being able to speak a few basic Arabic words will make your vacation more enjoyable and show that you understand the local way of life. Common Arabic phrases to know are "marhaban" (hello), "shukran" (thank you), "afwan" (you're welcome), and "ma'a as-salama" (goodbye).

Translation Apps: Phrasebooks and translation apps can be useful tools for travelers to utilize during conversations with persons they might not know well in English or who are traveling in unfamiliar territory.

12.3 Tipping Customs: Thanking Others for Helped Services

Tipping is required and usual in Egypt for certain services. Tipping amounts may vary depending on the level of service received and the traveler's budget, but it's important to recognize and appreciate the efforts of service providers.

- Restaurants: A 10%–15% service charge may be added to the bill in restaurants. If there is no service fee, it is customary to leave a tip of 10%–15% of the total amount. Additionally, it's appreciated if you leave the wait staff with a little change or round up the amount.

Hotels: Tipping hotel staff, such as housekeepers, bellhops, and concierges, is customary in Egypt. It is usual to tip housekeeping staff 10–20 EGP every night, while bellboys can receive 5–10 EGP per bag for assistance with luggage. Tipping is customary when drivers and tour guides deliver exceptional service.

Transportation: Taxi drivers are appreciative of clients who round up or leave a little tip for exceptional service, even if they don't request gratuities. Tipping for longer journeys or private drivers often ranges from 10 to 20 EGP.

12.4 Local Customs and Etiquette: Respecting Egyptian Traditions

Visitors to Egypt should be cognizant of and respectful of the customs and manners of the people, as this fosters cultural sensitivity and strengthens ties with the community.

Clothing: Given that Muslims make up the majority of Egypt's population, modest clothing is recommended, especially when visiting holy sites or rural areas. Western-style clothing is fine in cities and tourist destinations, but tourists should observe local customs by covering their shoulders and knees.

- Public Behavior: It is advisable to refrain from making frequent public displays of affection because Egyptian culture discourages intimacy in public. Additionally, guests should refrain from voicing their ire or dissatisfaction in public as it is greatly valued to act calmly and politely.

Photography: It is important to get permission before taking images of individuals, especially locals, in order to respect their privacy and cultural values. Additionally, it's a good idea to confirm before snapping photos in places of worship or the military, as some may prohibit or restrict photography.

- Greetings: When extending a greeting, people of the same gender should shake hands. Men and women often do not shake hands, though this could differ depending on individual preferences and level of familiarity.

To sum up, having practical knowledge regarding currency conversion, basic Arabic communication, tipping, and local etiquette can all make a big difference in your vacation to Egypt. By accepting cultural differences with openness and respect, travelers can develop lasting memories of their time in this enticing location, handle daily life with ease, and form meaningful friendships with locals.

13. CONSCIENTIOUS TRAVEL AND SUSTAINABILITY

In recent times, the global tourism industry has placed greater emphasis on sustainability and ethical conduct, acknowledging the need of preserving natural resources, protecting cultural heritage, and supporting local communities. Sustainable development and responsible tourism are crucial to preserving Egypt's rich cultural past, diverse ecosystems, and well-known landmarks for future generations. This large book explores the ecotourism initiatives, responsible travel practices, and community engagement initiatives that support Egypt's tourist industry's sustainable growth.

13.1 Ecotourism Initiatives: Preserving Natural Wonders and Biodiversity

Egypt's ecotourism initiatives aim to support conservation efforts, promote environmentally responsible travel practices that lessen harm to the environment, and raise public awareness of the importance of safeguarding the nation's natural resources. These initiatives, which range from animal reserves and eco-friendly hotels to protected areas and sustainable tourism projects, show Egypt's commitment to the growth of sustainable tourism.

- Protected Areas: Egypt has a number of national parks and protected areas that preserve its distinctive natural ecosystems and wildlife. These are the Saint Katherine Protectorate in South Sinai, the Red Sea Governorate's Wadi El Gamal National Park, and the Sinai Peninsula's Ras Mohammed National Park. These protected areas support conservation efforts and sustainable tourism practices while providing opportunities for environmentally friendly activities including hiking, birdwatching, and wildlife viewing.

Conservation of Coral Reefs: The Red Sea is well known for its colorful coral reefs, which are home to a wide variety of marine life. Sustainable diving practices, marine conservation, and coral reef conservation are the main focuses of Red Sea ecotourism programs. The goal of initiatives like marine conservation education, coral restoration, and reef monitoring is to protect the richness and health of the Red Sea's coral reefs for coming generations.

- Community-Based Tourism: By protecting their natural resources and cultural legacy, local communities are empowered to reap the benefits of tourism. Through initiatives like homestays, cultural tours, and handicraft workshops, tourists may interact with locals, discover their customs, and promote sustainable livelihoods. Egypt hopes to guarantee that tourism helps locals and contributes to the reduction of poverty and economic growth of rural areas by encouraging community-based tourism.

13.2 Conscious Travel: Reducing Pollution and Encouraging Cultural Understanding

In Egypt, responsible travel focuses on preserving the environment, honoring regional cultures, and encouraging the growth of a sustainable tourism industry. By implementing conscientious travel strategies, tourists can play a part in preserving the environment, safeguarding cultural assets, and assisting local communities.

- Reduce, Reuse, Recycle: By cutting back on waste, using less water and energy, and disposing of garbage properly, travelers may lessen their impact on the environment. While minimizing environmental effect and conserving water and electricity in lodgings and natural habitats can help reduce plastic waste, bringing reusable water bottles, shopping bags, and toiletries can also assist reduce plastic waste.

- Respect Cultural Heritage: Egypt has a rich cultural legacy that should be handled with reverence and respect. This includes ancient monuments, archeological sites, and religious sites. When visiting cultural sites, visitors should abide by the rules and regulations, stay off of unstable items, and not engage in disruptive activities like littering, vandalism, or graffiti. Travelers may contribute to the preservation of Egypt's riches for the enjoyment of future generations by respecting cultural heritage.

- Support Local Communities: Through responsible tourist practices, local communities can be supported, and this can benefit livelihoods, economic growth, and cultural preservation. In addition to participating in community-based tourism programs and exchanging cultures with locals, tourists can also support local businesses, craftsmen, and tour operators. Responsible tourists can support Egypt's efforts to reduce poverty and establish a sustainable tourism industry by empowering local economies and communities.

13.3 Encouraging Local Communities: Providing Residents with Empowerment and Fostering Inclusivity

One of the main tenets of Egypt's sustainable tourism development is community support, which guarantees that visitors benefit locals and promotes equitable growth and economic prosperity. Travelers can contribute to the creation of chances for sustainable livelihoods, cultural preservation, and community empowerment by patronizing local shops, artisans, and entrepreneurs.

- Artisanal Crafts: Egypt boasts a rich history of producing jewelry, ceramics, weaving, and traditional needlework, among other artisanal crafts. By buying handcrafted goods and mementos, visiting artisan workshops and cooperatives, and discovering traditional workmanship, tourists can help local craftspeople. Travelers can contribute to the preservation of traditional skills and sustainable lives in rural communities by purchasing goods from local craftsmen.

- Culinary Tourism: While discovering Egypt's varied flavors and culinary traditions, culinary tourism gives chances to assist regional farmers, food producers, and small-scale food businesses. In addition to participating in cooking lessons and food tours, tourists can try traditional meals at neighborhood restaurants, street food vendors, and markets and learn about the culinary customs and cuisines of the area. Travelers may encourage cultural interchange, support regional food systems, and contribute to sustainable food production and consumption by adopting culinary tourism.

- Community-Based Tourism Initiatives: By protecting their natural resources and cultural legacy, local communities are empowered to engage in and profit from tourism. Homestays, cultural tours, and handicraft workshops are just a few of the genuine experiences that these programs provide to encourage cross-cultural dialogue, sustainable livelihoods, and community development. Travelers can learn about traditional ways of life, customs, and traditions while also promoting inclusive growth and economic development by interacting with local communities.

In conclusion, protecting Egypt's natural treasures, cultural legacy, and local communities for future generations depends heavily on sustainable and ethical tourism. Travelers may help Egypt's natural resources, cultural legacy, inclusive growth, and economic prosperity by supporting local communities, participating in ecotourism programs, and adopting responsible travel habits. Travelers may guarantee that tourism benefits current and future generations while maintaining the beauty and diversity of Egypt's landscapes, cultures, and communities by adopting sustainable tourism principles and showing respect for local customs and traditions.

14. EXTRA RESOURCES FOR VISITORS TO EGYPT

There is more to getting ready for a vacation to Egypt than just packing your bags and making travel plans. A seamless trip can be guaranteed and your travel experience can be substantially improved by having access to trustworthy information, practical resources, and emergency contacts. We'll cover a wide range of extra resources in this extensive guide for visitors to

Egypt, such as practical websites and applications, suggested reading lists to broaden your knowledge of Egypt's past and present, and crucial emergency contacts to keep on hand in the event of unanticipated events.

14.1 Helpful Websites and Applications: Obtaining Information Quickly

Travelers have a plethora of services and information at their fingertips in the digital age. These websites and apps may assist you in organizing and managing every part of your trip to Egypt, whether you're seeking for advice on where to go, how to get around, or how to use the local transit system.

The Tourism Authority of Egypt (ETA): The Egypt Tourism Authority's official website offers visitors to Egypt a wealth of information about places to visit, things to do, events, and useful travel advice. The ETA website is a fantastic tool for organizing your itinerary and finding hidden treasures, including everything from ancient sites and cultural icons to adventurous activities and dining experiences.

Maps on Google: An essential tool for exploring Egypt's villages, cities, and attractions is Google Maps. With its thorough maps, up-to-date traffic reports, and information on public transportation, Google Maps makes it simple to plan journeys, locate neighboring eateries and activities, and confidently explore new places.

- Booking.com: Booking.com is a well-known website that allows users to book a variety of lodgings in Egypt, including hotels, resorts, guesthouses, and apartments. Booking.com assists tourists in selecting the ideal lodging option based on their interests and budget by providing them with flexible booking options, user reviews, and images.

- XE Currency Converter: With its up-to-date conversion rates, XE Currency Converter is a useful tool for visitors visiting Egypt. XE Currency Converter assists you in staying up to date on currency conversion rates and making wise financial decisions whether you're buying at local markets or exchanging money at a bank.

- TripAdvisor: When it comes to restaurant recommendations, reviews, and insider information about Egypt's accommodations, hotels, and activities, TripAdvisor is a great resource. While visiting Egypt's fascinating locations, TripAdvisor's millions of user-generated reviews and ratings assist visitors in spotting the best experiences and avoiding tourist traps.

14.2 Suggested Reading: Expanding Your Knowledge of Egypt's Past and Present

These suggested reading selections will help you fully immerse yourself in Egypt's rich history, culture, and heritage. From modern literature and travel memoirs to ancient history and mythology, these books provide insights into Egypt's intriguing past and present.

- Richard H. Wilkinson's "The Complete Gods and Goddesses of Ancient Egypt": With the help of this thorough reference to the gods and goddesses that the ancient Egyptians worshipped, you may explore the realm of ancient Egyptian mythology and religion. A fascinating survey of Egyptian religious beliefs and rituals, this book features lesser-known gods and local spirits alongside more powerful deities like Ra and Isis.

- Ian Shaw, editor of "The Oxford History of Ancient Egypt": With the help of this reliable and comprehensible summary, learn about the history of ancient Egypt from its prehistoric beginnings to the conclusion of the Pharaonic era. Including essays by prominent Egyptologists, this book paints a complete picture of ancient Egyptian civilization by addressing a variety of subjects including politics, society, religion, art, and architecture.

- Lawrence Durrell's "The Alexandria Quartet": "The Alexandria Quartet" is a compelling examination of love, desire, and identity set against the backdrop of Egypt's cultural melting pot in the cosmopolitan city of Alexandria in the 1940s. Durrell paints a stunning picture of this dynamic city during a period of social and political revolution by evoking the sights, sounds, and atmosphere of Alexandria via the interwoven stories of its individuals.

Alaa Al Aswany's "The Yacoubian Building": This best-selling book, which is set in Cairo's famous Yacoubian Building, provides a broad overview of Egyptian culture via the experiences of its varied cast of people. "The Yacoubian Building" examines issues of class, corruption, and social inequality in modern Egypt, illuminating the complexity of Egyptian life from the perspective of wealthy aristocrats to struggling working-class citizens.

14.3 Emergency Contacts: Preserving Your Safety

It's crucial to make emergency plans and carry vital contact information with you when traveling in Egypt in case of unanticipated events. When you most need help, these emergency contacts can offer medical attention, police support, or assistance from the embassy.

Dial 122 for police assistance, 123 for medical emergencies (ambulance), and 180 for fire emergencies in order to access emergency services (police, ambulance, and fire).

- Police for Tourists: In addition to reporting crimes and lodging complaints, the Tourist Police (tel: 126) also offers assistance and support to visitors to Egypt, including details on tourist destinations and safety precautions.

- Consulates and Embassy: It is crucial to have the phone number of your nation's embassy or consulate in Egypt on hand in case of emergency. For help with passport problems, legal concerns, medical emergencies, and other consular services, get in touch with your embassy or consulate.

Insurance for Travel: Make sure you have sufficient travel insurance before visiting Egypt. This coverage should include emergency medical expenses, trip cancellation and interruption, and medical evacuation and repatriation.

To sum up, having access to helpful websites and apps, suggested reading lists and vital emergency contacts can improve your trip experience in Egypt and keep you connected, informed, and safe the entire time. Travelers can confidently plan their trips, gain a deeper understanding of Egypt's history and culture, and be ready for any unforeseen circumstances by making use of these resources. Egypt offers an abundance of experiences just waiting to be discovered, whether you choose to explore historic sites, navigate busy marketplaces, or become fully immersed in regional customs and traditions.

15. CONCLUSION

It's time to take stock of the amazing experiences, priceless memories, and enduring impressions this ancient land has left on you as your journey through Egypt comes to an end. Egypt has captured your heart and mind with its rich history, varied landscapes, and warm hospitality—from witnessing the pyramids' timeless beauty to fully immersing yourself in the lively culture of Cairo. In this last chapter, we wish visitors to Egypt a fond farewell and offer some last-minute suggestions and ideas for their final days there.

15.1 Concluding Advice and Suggestions: Getting the Most Out of Your Stay in Egypt

Here are some last tips and suggestions to ensure a smooth and enjoyable conclusion to your trip as you get ready to leave Egypt and head back home:

Allow Time for Introspection: Give yourself some time to think back on your travels and the understandings you gained from experiencing Egypt's history, culture, and natural beauty. Whether you journal about your experiences, share stories with other travelers, or just take a moment to take in the sights and sounds of your surroundings, thinking back on your journey will enhance your appreciation of this amazing place.

Enjoy the Tastes: Enjoy a few last bites of delicious food before leaving Egypt, ranging from authentic street food to upscale delicacies. Treat your taste buds to one last culinary adventure before departing, whether it's eating a magnificent feast of Egyptian cuisine at a fine dining restaurant or sampling falafel and koshary from a local market stall.

Note down Memories: Spend some time capturing enduring memories of your journey across Egypt through sketches, movies, or photos. Every picture captures a moment in time that you may cherish long after you've left and tells a story, whether it's of grand buildings and busy bazaars or serene landscapes and energetic street scenes.

Show Your Appreciation: Express gratitude to everyone who helped to make your stay in Egypt memorable, including the locals who greeted you with open arms and shared their culture and customs, the hotel staff who showed you their love and expertise for Egypt's history, and your tour guide. A heartfelt thank you and a pleasant gesture can go a long way in creating lasting connections and leaving a great impression.

15.2 Farewell to Egypt: Until We Meet Again

Take a moment to relish the sights, sounds, and experiences of this incredible place one final time before saying goodbye to Egypt. Egypt's timeless beauties, from the mighty pyramids of Giza to the serene waters of the Nile, will linger in your memory, beckoning you to return and rediscover their beauty and mystique.

Take the spirit of Egypt—its tenacity, diversity, and enduring legacy—with you on your journey home. May the memories of your trip to this ancient land inspire and enhance your life for years to come, whether you decide to revisit Egypt or tell friends and family about your experiences.

Egypt, good bye till we cross paths again under the desert's golden sun, next to the Nile's timeless waters, and amid the historical echoes that reverberate throughout your ancient land. May the wonders of Egypt accompany you on your journey and become a treasured memory of your epic trek through life as you move forward.

In summary, Egypt provides visitors with an amazing voyage through history, tradition, and humanity. It is a country of timeless wonders, vibrant culture, and friendly hospitality. Egypt captivates the imagination and makes a lasting impression on those who visit, whether they choose to explore ancient structures, cruise the Nile, or become fully immersed in local customs and traditions. When you say goodbye to Egypt, take with you the knowledge, insights, and experiences gained from your voyage, and let the essence of this amazing place to inspire and enhance your life no matter where your travels may take you.

Made in United States
Orlando, FL
25 January 2025

57764856R00041